Sewing for CHRISTMAS

Concentration Level

 Nice and relaxing... let's day dream

 This is fun

 Mmmm, let's think

Put the coffee on, white no sugar

Florrie's things to remember list

Real Christmas tree

Family together

Carols around the piano

Bullets (the sweet kind)

Surprises

Silk stockings

A sober Betty

Peace

Betty's Christmas Present List

Handmade gifts

Bottle of Sherry

Jar of Bah Humbugs

New Glasses

Annual pass for Beamish

Fondant for the Bees

Lace trimmed smalls

A knees up

Homespun Christmas Garland

Garlands are used on most festive occasions around the world. Inspired by the paper garlands of old, our Christmas garland looks perfect in so many locations, for example around a tree or decorating a fireplace, window or door.

What you need

Felt for Stars 10cms (4")	Green Fabric 20cms (8")
Felt for Stockings 10cms (4")	1.5m Paper twine
Scraps of Felt for Berries	1m Ribbon
Red Fabric 30cms (12")	Toy Filling

Finished Size: 1 metre long approx.

How to make it

Make templates of a stocking, star, holly leaf, stocking top and a berry on page 16.

Stockings; fold the red fabric WST and trace around the template 6 times, cut on this line. Trace the stocking top template 6 times onto the felt and cut on the line.

For stockings place the felt onto the stocking, **see photo** for placement and pin in place. Or if you wish to decorate them do it now, using embellishments, decorative stitches, even add the names of your family. When you have finished decorating sew around the stocking leaving the top open to add presents or toy filling. Make a hanging loop from ribbon and stitch to the top of the stocking.

Holly Leaves; fold the holly fabric WST and trace around the holly template 10 times. Cut out on this line. Sew around each leaf, we used a running stitch, leave a small gap and insert a small amount of toy filling. Sew the gap closed. Sew a running stitch up the centre of the leaf. Repeat for all the leaves. Now sew 2 leaves together and add berries made using the berry template. **See photo.**

Stars; using the star template cut out 4 stars. Place 2 together and sew around the edge using any stitch you desire, leave a small gap and insert toy filling, sew gap closed. Add a button if desired.

See photo for placement and sew each of the items to the paper twine. Make a loop at each end of the twine for hanging.

Once the Garland was up the first thing Betty would do is get her finest crystal glass from the cabinet and pour a large glass of Sloe Gin, sit in her favourite chair next the fire and admire her work.

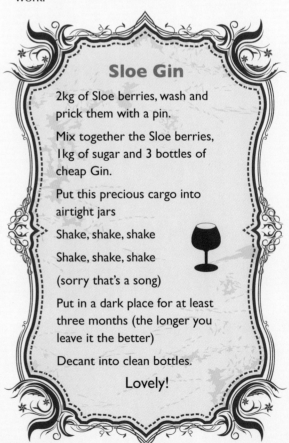

Sloe Gin

2kg of Sloe berries, wash and prick them with a pin.

Mix together the Sloe berries, 1kg of sugar and 3 bottles of cheap Gin.

Put this precious cargo into airtight jars

Shake, shake, shake

Shake, shake, shake

(sorry that's a song)

Put in a dark place for at least three months (the longer you leave it the better)

Decant into clean bottles.

Lovely!

QUOTES FROM FLORRIE

Cont....

We did a play at Chapel one Christmas and we all had to have costumes made. Well we had nothing and I remember I was a tree so Mam dressed me head to foot in green, thick woollen stockings I think they were, a long ganzy and me friend balaclava. She knotted strips of old fabrics together and draped them around me. I remember I wasn't happy; I wanted to be an angel.

They had a piano in one of the cottages. Their son was me friend and me and Kate used to gan over and have a sing song. Mrs Watson would give us biscuits and ginger beer and me favourite Christmas carol was 'In the bleak mid winter' His father used to play the piano and he was good at it, he used to jazz it up a bit and make us laugh.

Mam would make a Christmas cake in September. I was a lot younger than me sisters, they used to help Mam with the ingredients if she was struggling, not that she'd ever admit to that mind!

POLICE WARNI...

Sgt Biff has bee... offering some a... for the festive p... He is concerned... that the pastime... of 'clashing wo... lass after a sess... is unacceptable... Be warned that... perpetrators wi... shown the error... their ways'.

Shortbre... thief returns biscuits

A batch of fresh... baked shortbrea... mysteriously w... missing from th... kitchen of Miss... Betty. It was ini... thought they we... gone for good,... however, the ma... have since been... returned along... a note containin... baking tips and... br...denti...

3

Festive Stitched Stationary

Taking our inspiration from Victorian Christmas cards and embroidered postcards, these sweet little designs work well on cards and tags. You could also incorporate them into other Christmas projects.

What you need

Cream Fabric Fat 16th

Weaveline Fat 16th

Embroidery threads

Lace 1m

Beads, Buttons to embellish

Cardstock

Fabric Glue

Finished Size: Robin 5" x 7" and Wreath 3" x 3"

How to make it

Iron the Weaveline to the back of the cream fabric and trace the stitchery design of your choice on page 14.

Using 2 strands of embroidery thread, stitch the design using a back stitch and french knots. **See photo** for colours. Add beads and or buttons if desired. Trim the fabric for the Robin Stitchery to 8" x 6" and the wreath to 4" x 4".

Cut a piece of card for the Robin 7" x 5" and the Wreath 3" x 3".

Glue the stitched fabric to the card and fold the extra fabric to the back of the card and glue in place. Allow to dry.

See photo for placement and glue lace to the cards. Mount onto cardstock as desired and embellish.

Florrie used the small wreath design to make matching gift tags. If you look at the small photograph above, she has hung one on a decanter.

Snowflake Lap Quilt

Dreaming of a White Christmas? Keep warm and cosy with this simple lap quilt. Quick and easy to make and simply quilted with a snowflake design, this is an ideal project to for the festive season.

What you need

Red Fabric 1.9m

White Fabric 1.2m

Dark Green Fabric 30cms (12")

Light Green Fabric 30cms (12")

Wadding 1.5m

Backing 3m

Finished Size: 56" x 56" approx.

Cutting

Red Fabric cut 13 x 6⅞" x 6⅞" and cut 6 x 5½" strips WOF

White Fabric cut 52 x 3¼" squares cut in half on the diagonal and cut 12 x 9½" squares. 4 x 5½" squares.

Dark Green cut 26 x 2¾" squares and cut 26 x 2½" squares

Light Green cut 26 x 2¾" squares and cut 26 x 2½" squares

How to make it

Snowball Blocks. Place a 2¾" light green square onto the corner of a white 9½" white square. Draw a line on the diagonal and sew on this line. Cut away the excess green fabric but leave the white fabric underneath which will ensure your block stays square. Repeat with a light green fabric square on the opposite corner. Sew a dark green square in the same manner on the remaining 2 corners.

Repeat for the remaining 11 blocks, making a total of 12 Snowball blocks.

Square Block; sew a white triangle to each side of a 2½" light green square. **See photo**. Make a total of 26. Repeat using the dark green squares. Make a total of 26.

Sew a light green segment to one side of the red 6⅞" square, sew a light green segment to the opposite side of the square. Press and sew a dark green segment to the remaining 2 sides of the square. Make a total of 13 blocks.

Refer to the photo for placement and sew the Snowball squares, and the square blocks into rows.

Measure the sides of the quilt and cut the 5½" red borders to the correct size. Sew the side borders onto the quilt.

Now sew a 5½" white square to each end of the 2 remaining red borders and sew these to the quilt.

Layer the quilt top and quilt as desired. We have included a snowflake template on page 15 which we used in the snowball blocks. Bind the quilt using your preferred method or see the Work Basket.

Parcel Advent Calendar

We love Advent Calendars. Get ready for the big countdown with this fun wall hanging with 3d parcels. This calendar is suitable for boys and girls of all ages.

What you need

Cream Fabric 40cms (16")

Red Bow Fabric 30cms (12")

Red Border Fabric 10cms (4")

Red felt 10cms (4")

Assorted scraps for parcels & crackers

Heat 'n' Bond Ultra 10cms (4")

Scraps of foam or sponge approx ½" thickness

Wadding 50cms (20")

Backing 50cms (20")

Binding 20cms (8")

Finished Size: 17½" x 28½"

Cutting

Cream Fabric cut 2 x 7½" squares, 2 x 13½" x 7½"

Red Bow Fabric cut 1 x 3½" x 7½", 1 x 3½" x 13½", 1 x 15" x 8" and 1 x 9" x 4"

Red Border Fabric cut 2 x 17½" x 3½"

Red Felt cut 24 x 2" squares

Binding cut 3 x 2½" strips WOF

How to make it

Trace the numbers on page 14 onto the Heat 'n'Bond Ultra. Fuse the numbers onto the 2" felt squares. Use a cloth between the iron and felt to protect it.

Sew a cream 7½" square to each side of the 3½" x 7½" red bow fabric strip. Sew the remaining cream rectangles to each side of the 3½" x 13½" red bow fabric strip. Press to the red fabrics. Now sew a 3½" x 17½" red bow fabric strip to the bottom of the smaller panel, now add the remaining panel, **see photo** for placement.

Sew the border fabric to the top and bottom.

See photo for placement and pin the numbered squares in place. Stitch each of the sides and bottom of the squares, leave the tops open, this creates a pocket.

To make the bow fold the 15" x 8" fabric RST lengthwise. Sew around leaving a gap. Turn through and stuff firmly. Sew the gap closed by hand stitching. With the remaining bow fabric fold RST and sew leaving a small gap to turn through. Sew gap closed and press. Wrap this fabric around the stuffed bow, **see photo** and pull tightly, secure with stitching.

Make a number of assorted parcels and crackers. Cut the foam or sponge and wrap them in fabric. Secure the fabric by stitching on the reverse of the parcels & crackers. Add bows, buttons or embellishments, **see photo** for inspiration.

Layer the advent panel onto wadding and backing and quilt as desired. Bind as desired see Work Basket. Add tabs or a hanging sleeve, see Work Basket.

To complete the advent calendar position the bow, parcels and crackers, **see photo** and either glue or stitch them into place.

Sixpenny Table Centrepiece

Perfect for any occasion, this project looks fabulous on a Christmas table. The design is loosely based on a penny rug but with a modern twist and is quickly made from 2½" strips.

What you need

32 x 2½" assorted strips

Centre fabric 30cms (12")

H640 70cms (27")

Green fabric 10cms (4")

Scraps for berries

Finished Size: 17½" x 28½"

How to make it

Cut the 2½" strips into 8" lengths and sew them lengthwise into 16 pairs. Fuse H640 onto the reverse of 8 pairs. Place the remaining pairs RST, pin in place. Draw a 45° angle on each side of the centre seam, this makes a point. Sew around leaving the opposite end to the point open for turning. Cut off the excess fabric at the point and turn through, press.

Make a template by drawing around a dinner plate (10½" diameter). Cut 2 circles from the centre fabric and a slightly smaller circle from the H640.

Make 6 holly leaves and 9 berries using the templates on page 16. **See photo** and appliqué them onto one of the fabric circles. Once complete fuse the H640 to the reverse of this circle.

Turn under a ¼" hem around both circles and tack in place. Place the plain circle onto a table wrong side facing up and position the pairs evenly around, you need to ensure each pair overlaps the circle by half an inch. Place the appliquéd circle on the top, with the right side facing you, **see photo** for placement. Now pin and tack everything in place. Blanket stitch or use a decorative stitch of your choice to secure. Remove the tacking stitches.

Hark, is that the sleigh
I hear

Drawing closer, almost here

Piled so high with sacks of toys

For all the special girls and boys

Christmas is a time of love

For counting blessings from above

With tables laden full of food

And sherry wine to
help the mood

Felt Snowflakes

Our snowflakes are quick and easy to make. An ideal project for children or men of any age.

What you need

6" squares of white felt

Embellishments

What also might come in helpful

Large glass of Sloe Gin, see page 2

Finished Size: 5"

How to make it

To make the Snowflake make a template from page 15.

Cut out the snowflake from the felt. Pinch in each end and cut out assorted shapes, similar to paper cutting, **see photo.**

Embellish as desired. They can either be hung using fishing wire or invisible thread or use blue tack and fix to the window.

Rag Ball Robin

Christmas wouldn't be Christmas without seeing a Robin in the garden. But this makes a nice little addition to any Christmas table.

What you need

Assorted lengths of fabric ½" width, including brown to finish

Red Buttons & Beads

Scraps of black & green felt

Glue

Finished Size: 9½" in circumference

How to make it

To make the Rag Ball Robin wrap the fabric into a ball until it is approximately the size of a tennis ball. Make sure the last covering layers are a brown fabric. Glue ends down to secure.

Make a template of the beak and holly on page 15. and cut from black felt. **See photo** for placement. Add beads for eyes or you could use black headed pins. Glue buttons and beads to make the robins chest. Use the template on page 15 and cut out 3 holly leaves from green felt, glue them in place, add beads for decoration to the robin.

Templates & Work Basket

Quilting

Quilting stitches hold all three layers together and can create texture.

You can hand or machine quilt. If using a sewing machine increase the stitch length. Some machines have a setting which will automatically do this.

If sewing by hand use a quilting needle or between and do a running stitch through all 3 layers. Do not worry about doing small stitches it is better that all your stitches are the same length. The more you do the better you will get. Betty prefers to use a Quilt hoop available from your local quilting shop.

Hanging sleeve

A hanging sleeve on the back of your quilt makes it easier for hanging at home or in a quilt show.

Cut fabric 8″ wide and the width of your quilt.

Hem the short edges. Place RST and sew the long edge. Turn though and press the seam to the middle. Centre onto the top of the reverse of the quilt approx. ½″ from the binding and whipstitch in place.

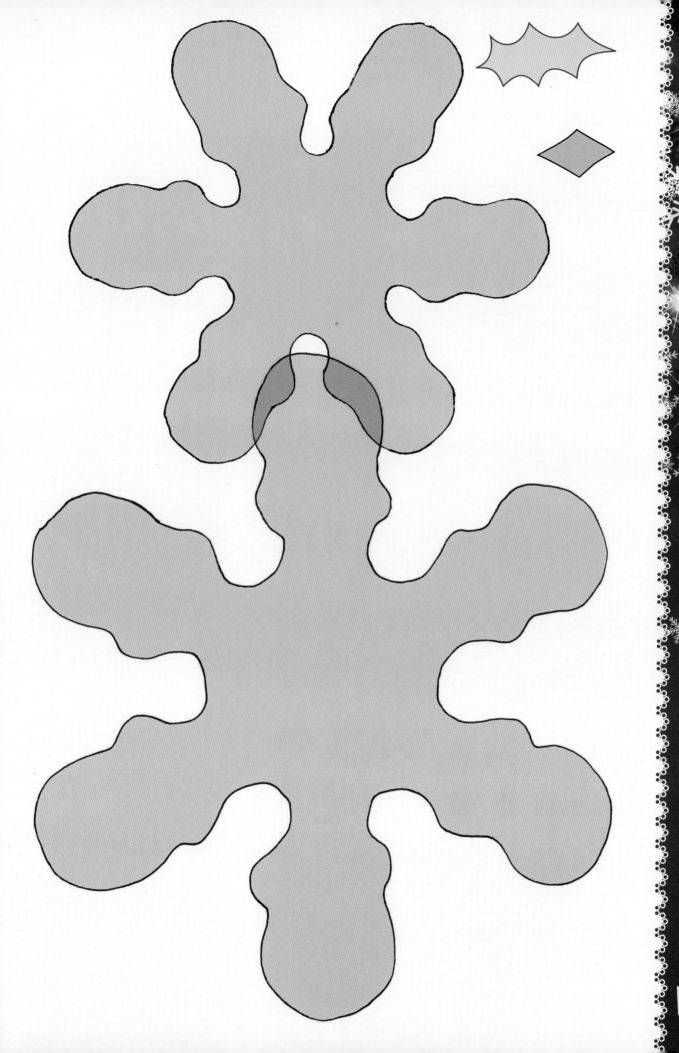

Templates & Work Basket

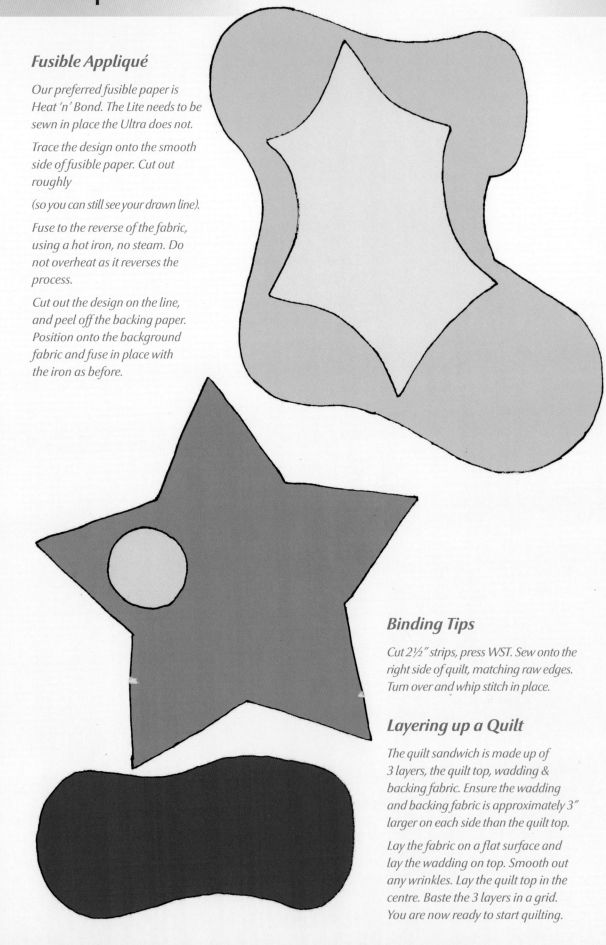

Fusible Appliqué

Our preferred fusible paper is Heat 'n' Bond. The Lite needs to be sewn in place the Ultra does not.

Trace the design onto the smooth side of fusible paper. Cut out roughly

(so you can still see your drawn line).

Fuse to the reverse of the fabric, using a hot iron, no steam. Do not overheat as it reverses the process.

Cut out the design on the line, and peel off the backing paper. Position onto the background fabric and fuse in place with the iron as before.

Binding Tips

Cut 2½" strips, press WST. Sew onto the right side of quilt, matching raw edges. Turn over and whip stitch in place.

Layering up a Quilt

The quilt sandwich is made up of 3 layers, the quilt top, wadding & backing fabric. Ensure the wadding and backing fabric is approximately 3" larger on each side than the quilt top.

Lay the fabric on a flat surface and lay the wadding on top. Smooth out any wrinkles. Lay the quilt top in the centre. Baste the 3 layers in a grid. You are now ready to start quilting.